COMPOSITION & CREATIVE WRITING

FOR THE MIDDLE GRADES

by Imogene Forte
and
Joy MacKenzie

Incentive Publications, Inc.
Nashville, Tennessee

Illustrated by Kathleen Bullock
Cover by Geoffrey Brittingham

ISBN 0-86530-176-X

TABLE OF CONTENTS

PREFACE

COMPOSITION AND CREATIVE WRITING is a remarkably bare-bones, ordinary title for a book that champions the unique, the imaginative, and the inventive in written expression, but it employs an even more important element of good writing – it is precise! We want you to know that what these pages have to offer you and your middle grade students is a stunning, practical collection of exciting activities for developing writing skills that are basic to the process of original, personal communication.

In a world of cable TV, cellular phones, telecommunication satellites, and computerized printing; selling, banking, buying, and gaming, who needs writing skills? Everybody, that's who! Technology has made great strides toward progress in the dissemination of ideas, but it has not been able to do it without words! Written language is still at the root of the whole communication process. Perhaps more than ever before in history, young people need the self-satisfaction and security of personal skill in communication to be able to articulate what they believe or feel, to enjoy the rewards of putting themselves and their ideas into whole, carefully-considered written form, to become people who are sensitive to themselves and their worlds and to the power of their language.

COMPOSITION AND CREATIVE WRITING was created to facilitate fluency, flexibility, and originality in the written communication skills of middle grade students. The format includes both teacher-directed lessons and independent student activity pages and is sequentially organized in keeping with the stages of the writing process. These complete lessons are presented in motivational settings designed to intrigue middle graders and sharpen their skills in specific areas of the writing process: collecting words and refining word usage, collecting and organizing ideas, perfecting technical writing skills, using literary forms, devices and figures of speech, editing, and proofreading.

The central focus of the book is that of helping middle grade students increase their love of language, their communication skills, and their sense of self-worth as they combine freedom of expression with the discipline of creating and perfecting a written piece. COMPOSITION AND CREATIVE WRITING FOR THE MIDDLE GRADES simplifies and expedites the achievement of these goals and makes the process exciting and challenging for both teacher and student!

THE BOA THAT BURST

PURPOSE:
Sequencing a story line

PREPARATION:

1. Write the following words (or 5 nouns and 5 verbs of your choosing) on the chalkboard in this format:

1. bus
2. turtle
3. coffeepot
4. dictionary
5. boa

6. burst
7. cried
8. danced
9. flew
10. crowed

2. Beneath these words, write:

The _____ That _____

3. Cover this section of the board from the students' view.

4. Supply each student with paper and pencils.

PROCEDURE:

1. Divide students into four or five groups.

2. Ask each student to choose a number between 1 and 5 and write it at the top of the paper. Then, ask each student to choose a second number between 6 and 10 and write that number beside the first number chosen.

3. Uncover the words on the board. Direct students to copy the title you placed on the board at the top of their papers, filling in the blanks with the words from the board that correspond to the numbers chosen.

Example: If a student chooses numbers 5 and 6, the title will be "The Boa That Burst."

4. Each student then begins to write about his/her title. After a few minutes, a signal is given, and papers are passed to the right. Each story is then continued by the next student. This process is repeated until everyone in each group has contributed to each story. On the final pass, students must bring the stories to a conclusion.

5. Taking turns, each student reads aloud the story for which he/she has written the conclusion.

THE WORD CO-OP

PURPOSE:
Collecting imaginative vocabulary

PREPARATION:

1. Prepare a large bulletin board area to resemble the model above. Include as many categories of words as space and interests/abilities of students allow.

2. Cut out 1" x 5" construction paper or tagboard strips on which to write the words.

3. Provide a box or envelope near the board for word strips and several markers.

THE WORD CO-OP

PROCEDURE:

1. Introduce to students the concept of a co-op (cooperative) store – owned and operated by and for the mutual benefit of all the customer-members.

2. Explain that they will all be members of a co-op that distributes words and that each of them will contribute to and borrow from the store on a regular basis.

3. Introduce the word categories and explain that it is each student's responsibility to contribute at least five words per day to the store. Encourage them to use their own imaginative resources as well as word resource books to gather their contributions. Certain categories may be specified each day, or the entire store can be open to receive words in any category.

Note: This assignment can be in effect for as long as is appropriate for the given circumstance but should be no shorter than a week.

4. In return for their contributions, students may use this vast store of words as a resource for writing assignments and their own personal writing.

5. Teachers should encourage students to take advantage of the store by making short daily assignments that require the use of the word co-op to create stories, poems, paragraphs, etc., that employ imagery, figurative language, and literary devices such as mood, emotional appeal, point of view, etc.

—————————————— **WORDS TO USE:** ——————————————

friendly	suspense	appreciation
unfriendly	size	soft
peace	disappointed	hard
war	season	nonsense
day	night	annoying
taste	repulsive	family
country	city	sports
pizzazz	music	nature
cold	sad	fear
warm	caution	fashion

PUT-TOGETHER PUZZLE

Name _____

One of the most challenging and exciting parts of writing is collecting the information you need to write. Often, getting the facts together is like working a gigantic puzzle. The following pages contain sample documents and personal references from the file of a person unknown to you, but one of whom you, as a police reporter, must write a description. Look carefully at the material. Learn all you can from it; then complete the two lists below.

✏ FACTS ABOUT THIS PERSON	FURTHER PERSONAL CONJECTURE AND OPINIONS RELATED TO THIS PERSON
1. _____	1. _____
2. _____	2. _____
3. _____	3. _____
4. _____	4. _____
5. _____	5. _____
6. _____	6. _____
7. _____	7. _____
8. _____	8. _____

Using the information you have now gathered, write as complete a description as possible of this person.

_____

_____

_____

_____

_____

_____

_____

_____

PUT-TOGETHER PUZZLE

Mrs. Adelle Ashcroft
8 Ashbury Alley
Adelaide, Australia
12345

Abe,

    J have tried for several years to locate you. Your
r Alex gave us your address in Africa, but our
o you there was returned marked "unknown." We
aced you to Athens and Arabia and we were told
d been in each place only briefly. Jt is good finally
e located your friend Asia in Atlanta and learn that
ere well.

    We shall look forward to meeting you upon your
from Aruba.

rely,
e

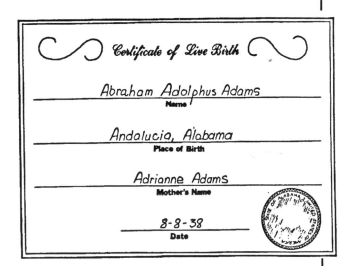

Certificate of Live Birth

Abraham Adolphus Adams
Name

Andalucia, Alabama
Place of Birth

Adrianne Adams
Mother's Name

8-8-38
Date

CT APPLES
E ADAMS

APPLICATION FOR EMPLOYMENT

Name   Adams   Abe   A.   Soc. Security No.   888-000-888
        Last   First   Middle Int.

Present Address   80 Allen Ave.   Anchorage   Alaska   99801
              No.   Street   City   State   Zip

How long have you lived at present address?   6 Months   Phone   614-888-4838

Previous Address   800 Ambrose Ave.   Anderson   AZ   85079
             No.   Street   City   State   Zip

How long did you live there?   3 Months   Date of Birth   8/8/38

Place of Birth   Andalucia, Alabama

EDUCATION

Elementary: Last grade completed   6
High School: Last grade completed   12
College: How many years completed?   6   Date of completion   1962
           Degree earned   M. A.   Date of completion _____
           Degree earned _____   Date of completion _____
           College Major   Foreign   College Minors   English
                      Languages   History
                                            Psychology

Interests, hobbies, or honors: Honors: Foreign Language Award; Lang. Society
  president; reading, traveling, backpacking, carpentry

PRIVATE EYE

PURPOSE:
Collecting information by observation

PREPARATION:

1. See that each student has a small notebook and a pencil to be used only for recording observations.

2. Make a copy of THE PRIVATE EYE'S GUIDE TO OBSERVATION work sheet for each student.

PROCEDURE:

1. Direct students to secretly choose one classmate as a "suspect" to "tail" or keep track of – "on the sly," of course.
Alternative: Students can draw names, or names can be assigned by the teacher.

2. Explain to the students that they should carefully observe as much of the daily activity of their suspect as possible and record all pertinent information in their "Private Eye" notebooks. THE PRIVATE EYE'S GUIDE TO OBSERVATION will suggest specific things to look for. Discuss the use of the guide, and caution students to avoid reference to physical characteristics and to be very careful that information is not hurtful or derogatory in any way.

3. At an appropriate time, each "Private Eye" prepares a summary report on his/her "suspect" and reads it to the class. If the "suspect" recognizes himself/herself from the description, he/she may reveal his/her identity. If not, the class can guess the "suspect's" identity.

THE PRIVATE EYE'S
GUIDE TO OBSERVATION

Name _____

      These open-ended statements are designed to help you observe your "suspect" in more detail. If you can complete all or most of these sentences, you will have recorded some very important specific information. Use wisely what you have learned to make your report.

The "SUSPECT"...

Is known by these aliases _____

_____

Is often seen _____

Spends a lot of time _____

Has a daily routine that includes such suspicious behaviors as_____

_____

Seems unusually intrigued by _____

Exhibits such unusual habits as _____

_____

Seems especially fond of _____

Can be most readily identified by _____

Is well-known for_____

Is very good at _____

Frequent companions are _____

Most likeable characteristic is _____

Most outstanding characteristic is _____

_____

Collecting Information By Observation
© 1991 by Incentive Publications, Inc., Nashville, TN.

SAIL A STORY

Name _____

Each island below represents a part of a story. Read each part carefully. Then, beginning with the island that starts the story, sail through the story by drawing a line to show the path of your ship as it connects the islands in proper order.

There may be more than one correct way to complete the connections. Choose the path that makes the story flow best and read most interestingly for you. Be ready to explain your choice. BEWARE! There is one island that does not seem to belong in this story. Sail on by – don't stop there at all!

No…it was only the incidental effect of another slumbering creature's natural behavior.

What was happening? Who or what could be responsible for this violent interruption of morning calm?

Was it nuclear war? An earthquake? Had a volcano erupted in the belly of the bay? Perhaps Big Foot had parachuted in from the Northwest!

Thousands of people were jerked awake by the nauseating, undulating motion that set solid, flat surfaces rolling in sea-like waves and caused tall buildings to bend and sway like giant Gumbies.

The dark, restless monster who lives deep in the earth's San Andreas fault had only coughed and turned over in his great, cavernous bed! All was well!

The sun glanced sideways at the placid scene and smiled.

But at 5:49 a.m., a vibrating jolt brought a sudden end to the peaceful slumber of the city's citizens.

A quiet, gray fog crept over the still-sleeping city of San Francisco.

Sequencing A Story Line
© 1991 by Incentive Publications, Inc., Nashville, TN.

SAIL A STORY!

Name _____

This is a children's story for you to write. First, look carefully at the picture for each part of the story. Decide which part should begin the story. Write the words for that part. Continue by locating the second part and writing words for it. Search your personal vocabulary for exciting, unusually descriptive words that will make each part fun to read. Keep going until you have finished the story. Then, number the parts in order so that your friends can read your story.

_____
(Write your title here.)

HEE HEE

SNAP

S-T-R-E-T-C-H

STRETCH A SENTENCE

PURPOSE:
Organizing and expanding ideas

PREPARATION:

1. Divide the class into evenly-matched teams.

PROCEDURE:

1. The first person on each team makes up a three-word sentence and recites it loudly and clearly.

2. The second person on the team then repeats that three-word sentence. If he/she does so accurately, the student then adds a fourth word anywhere in the sentence and recites that four-word sentence aloud.

3. The third person repeats the four-word sentence and then adds a fifth word. The activity continues in this manner until all team members have had a turn. (If a team member is unable to repeat a sentence, that turn is lost.) The team with the highest number of words in one sentence wins.

PARAPHRASE CRAZY

Name _____

Haste Makes Waste!

Can you rephrase that (say it in different words without changing the meaning)?

Hurrying causes error.
Or, if you hurry, you could make a mistake and have to start over, thus wasting time, energy, and materials.

Saying the same thing in different words is called paraphrasing. Usually, paraphrasing is done to make something more easily understood.

Trade these "antique" phrases for a translation written in your own modern language. Read each of the sentences below and paraphrase it. Then, write your paraphrase on the matching, newer item.

From whence cometh thou?

_____

Pray thee, draw nigh.

_____

Thy love will wane in due time.

_____

Would that he should welcome thy coming.

_____

Discretion is the better part of valor.

_____

Naught could assuage this fearful pain.

_____

This bloody task hath befallen me.

_____

Wilt thou meet me straightaway?

SUBTRACT FOR AN AD

Name _____

Developing the ability to "zero in" on just the most important facts of a story or news item is essential to good writing. The classified ad section of a newspaper is an excellent example of well-prepared or "précis" writing style because people pay for ads by the line. The shorter the ad, the less it costs!

Read some newspaper ads. Then try to copy that style by writing a classified ad that you think would sell each of the items shown below. Pretend that it costs you $10 a line! See how few lines you can use and still describe each item fully. Mention all the important details and point out the special features that will make people want to buy it.

A SPORTING AFFAIR

PURPOSE:
Using descriptive and action words

PREPARATION:

1. Participants will need paper and pencil.

PROCEDURE:

1. Select a sport in which the students are interested. Lead a group discussion about the sport, and list on the chalkboard at least a dozen descriptive words and a dozen action words related to that sport.

2. Direct students to write at least six well-constructed sentences related to the sport. Each sentence must contain one or more descriptive and action words.

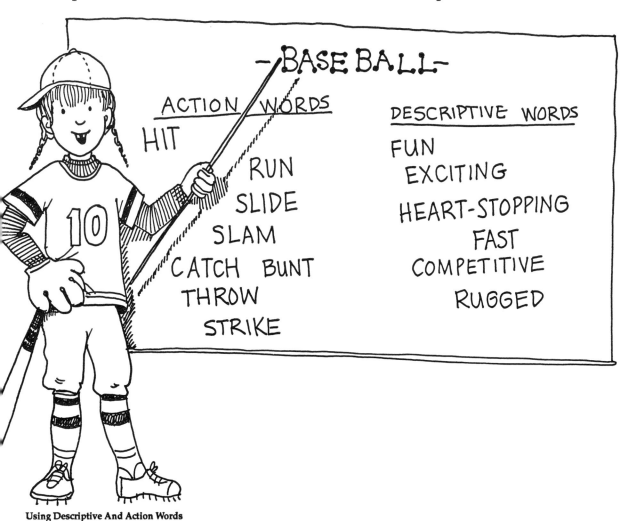

- BASEBALL -

ACTION WORDS
HIT
RUN
SLIDE
SLAM
CATCH BUNT
THROW
STRIKE

DESCRIPTIVE WORDS
FUN
EXCITING
HEART-STOPPING
FAST
COMPETITIVE
RUGGED

CATCH A CLICHÉ

PURPOSE:
Avoiding clichés

PREPARATION:

1. Reproduce copies of the FANCY FEATHERS story.

2. Prepare a list of commonly used clichés for use in class discussion (these could be printed on a chart or on the chalkboard).

PROCEDURE:

1. Lead a class discussion about clichés asking students to supply familiar ones.

2. In the discussion, point out that clichés are perhaps interesting when they are first used, but after a while, they become boring due to repetition.

3. Distribute the FANCY FEATHERS story, and direct students to circle all the clichés in the story.

4. After the clichés have been circled, direct students to work in small groups (no more than 4 or 5 in a group) to rewrite the story, avoiding clichés by using more interesting figurative language. One student in each group should be appointed secretary to write the story as others discuss and dictate.

5. Display the completed stories on a bulletin board, or share them orally to demonstrate differences in language usage and writing styles.

• from A to Z. from the bottom of my heart.

• wise as an owl.

Pretty as a picture.

high as a kite. proud as a peacock

FANCY FEATHERS

Name _____

Betsy Bluebird was as snug as a bug in a rug living with her mother and three sisters. Proud as a peacock, she preened and strutted as if her beautiful feathers had surely cost a pretty penny. In fact, old Mr. Owl said she behaved as if she had been born with a silver spoon in her mouth.

Early one morning while flitting from bush to bush she met Robin Red Breast, a dashing, fine-feathered friend. He being naively unaware that all that glitters is not gold invited her to tea. Quick as a wink she accepted.

Since they were able to see eye to eye, they immediately fell head over heels in love. They vowed to stick together through thick and thin and to face the music of life together. Robin said he would leave no stone unturned in his attempt to make Betsy happy, and she promised to lend an ear always when he needed a friend.

Their first problem arose when he suggested that they kill two birds with one stone by building their nest in Robin's territory while they were still young as spring chickens. Betsy began to cry crocodile tears and said her mother had always told her that birds of a feather flock together, and she really wanted to feather her nest near other bluebirds!

After much discussion, they finally came to a meeting of the minds and decided to compromise by building their first nest in a halfway tree. Since time flies, even for love birds, they let no grass grow under their feet and got started right away.

There are at least 20 clichés. How many did you find? _____

PRECISELY, MY DEAR

Name _____

Look at each picture below. In the first space provided by each one, write a noun from your own vocabulary which you feel accurately describes the idea or feeling in the picture.

_____

_____

_____

_____

_____

_____

_____

_____

_____

Now, look at the words written upside down at the bottom of this page. Assign each one to the picture which you feel it best labels or describes. (Use your dictionary to determine accurate word meanings.)

lunacy, fantasy, security, sentimentality, clemency

Making Precise Word Choices
© 1991 by Incentive Publications, Inc., Nashville, TN.

A WRITING BEE

PURPOSE:
Expanding word choices

PREPARATION:

1. Gather the following materials.
- scissors
- construction paper
- coffee stirrers or straws
- masking tape
- paper and pencils
- dictionaries

2. Use the pattern to create a large number of bees.

3. On each bee, write one descriptive word suitable to the level of the students.

4. Use masking tape to attach each bee to a drinking straw.

PROCEDURE:

1. Give each student a bee.

2. At a given signal, students send the bees into flight, tossing them into the air like paper airplanes.

3. When the bees land, each student picks up the nearest bee, reads the word on it, and writes a sentence using that word appropriately. At the end of the sentence, he/she writes in parentheses an additional word that is a synonym and could be used to replace the original descriptive word in his/her sentence.

4. At the next signal, all bees are again sent into flight.

5. Repeat this procedure until the students have used at least 8-10 words.

NOSE FOR NOISE

Name _____

Circle at least ten noisemakers in this picture.

On the lines in Column A, write one word for the sound each noisemaker might make. Be imaginative!

	A	B		A	B
1.	crying	bawling	6.		
2.			7.		
3.			8.		
4.			9.		
5.			10.		

Now, stretch your word power. Use the lines in Column B to write another sound word that could be identified with that noise.

───────── BONUS: ─────────

On a separate sheet of paper, use as many of the above sound words as possible in a paragraph. Give your paragraph a "sound" title!

Expanding Word Choices
© 1991 by Incentive Publications, Inc., Nashville, TN.

PLAY ON WORDS

PURPOSE:
Expanding word choices

PREPARATION:

1. Provide several sets of anagrams (Scrabble® game sets, ABC block sets, large homemade letter sets on cardboard squares, poker chips, plastic spoons, etc.).

2. For flexibility, several blanks may be included to be used in place of **any** letter.

PROCEDURE:

1. Divide students into teams of three or four.

2. Provide a set of anagrams for each team.

3. Explain that you will dictate and write on the chalkboard a single word that is normally overused by middle graders in their writing. Upon signal, each member of every team thinks of a synonym for the dictated word and quickly spells it out in anagrams. (No two members of the same team may use the same word.)

4. When all members of a team have successfully laid out a word, they signal by clasping hands and raising them together.

5. Their contributions may be written on the board opposite the original dictated word; then the team is awarded one point for each correctly used and correctly spelled word. (The teacher or student may keep score.)

6. The team with the most points at the end of the game wins.

Note: If time allows, additional synonyms contributed by other teams may be added to the board, and all participants may be asked to copy the words in their journals or writer's notebooks for future reference.

WORDS TO USE:

interesting	wonderful	beautiful
said	went	big
scared	bad	bright
fast	fat	ugly
get	good	happy
make	old	tell

WHAT'S IN THE BAG?

compact —
useful —
hand-held —
circular —
sharp —

— Give up?
It's a can opener.

PURPOSE:
Finding alternatives for
overused words

PREPARATION:

1. At the beginning of the week, decide with the students on a day for this activity to be presented.

PROCEDURE:

1. Each student brings one common household object of his/her choice to school in a small brown paper bag. The student's name should be written on the bottom of the bag so that it does not show.

2. Place all bags in a row.

3. Each person takes one bag, looks inside, and makes a list of five words that can be used to describe the object in the bag and/or tell for what purpose it is used. Encourage students to avoid the obvious or usual words that describe the objects.

4. Each student then holds his/her chosen bag closed before the group and gives the five words. Other group members try to guess what the item is. The person who guesses correctly gets the next turn. (It's fun when the person who brought the item can't guess, "What's in the bag!")

ADD A LITTLE COLOR

Name _____

    Lazy writers tend to use the same words over and over because it takes more effort to think of new or different ones. Have you ever found yourself using a word you know how to spell rather than looking up another one in the dictionary?

    Just to get started on an exciting approach to writing, use a dictionary or a thesaurus to find a more colorful word for each of the italicized words in the paragraph below. Recopy the paragraph with your replacement words in the space provided.

    Thunder *roared* and lightning *flashed* in the *dark* sky. *Big* gusts of wind blew *large* tree branches and *loose* boards around the *old* house. *Dark* clouds gathered and began to *drop* rain on the *dry* ground turning it into *brown* mud. An old man ran up the wet sidewalk to the old house. When he reached the *covered* porch, he turned around to *look* at the *big* storm. The rain was *coming* down in such *thick* sheets that he couldn't see the *curving* street in front of the house. He *looked* at the *heavy* rain and the *dark* clouds and *wished* that the *big* storm would *go away*. Then he shook his head, opened the *heavy* door, and *went* quietly inside.

    Compare the two paragraphs. List three additional words that could have been used somewhere in the paragraph to make it still more interesting.

_____   _____   _____

Finding Alternatives For Overused Words
© 1991 by Incentive Publications, Inc., Nashville, TN.

UNWANTED: WORN-OUT WORDS

Name _____

Here are ten tired, worn-out adjectives that need to be replaced by fresh, alive, more exact ones. Select one or two substitute words from Column B for each of the worn-out words in *italics*. Write the new adjectives you have selected for each word in the spaces provided in Column C.

A	B	C
1. *great* idea	splendid helpful	1) _____ idea
2. *nice* feeling	noble profitable	2) _____ feeling
3. *cute* girl	first-rate dreadful	3) _____ girl
4. *terrible* accident	disagreeable peculiar	4) _____ accident
5. *bad* storm	loyal horrendous	5) _____ storm
6. *fine* friend	delightful frightening	6) _____ friend
7. *funny* noise	strange superb	7) _____ noise
8. *big* house	terrific matchless	8) _____ house
9. *good* book	unpalatable expansive	9) _____ book
10. *awful* food	cherished satisfying grand superior sensational magnificent colossal attractive	10) _____ food

Nice pizza.

Incredible pizza!

Select one of the phrases you have created in Column C to use as a title for a short story. Write it on the back of this paper. Do not use any of the ten adjectives in Column A!

Finding Alternatives For Overused Words
© 1991 by Incentive Publications, Inc., Nashville, TN.

COMIN' ON STRONG!

Name _____

In the broadcasting world, information is sent by signal. The stronger the signal, the farther the message can be sent.

A writer's vocabulary is like a broadcast signal. The stronger it is, the farther the writer is likely to relay a message.

Strengthen your signal by finding as many precise synonyms for these overworked words as possible.

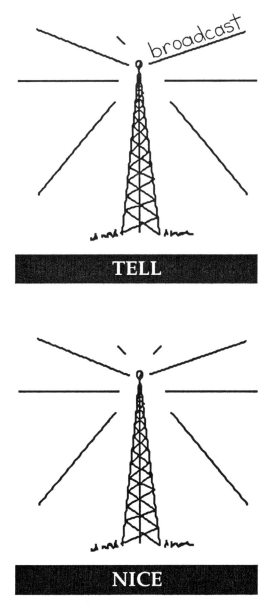

TELL

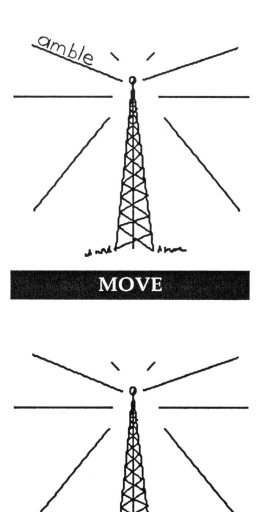

MOVE

NICE

OK

U FO s
(UNIDENTIFIED FIGURES OF SPEECH!)

Name _____

Concentrate your laser-powered, literary focus beam on these UFOs to see if you can identify them with one of these friendly alien groups:

(S) Simile   (M) Metaphor   (A) Alliteration

(O) Onomatopoeia   (P) Personification

Mark each UFO with its identifying initial shield. (A few UFOs may be members of more than one group!)

...Where winds the winsome wind......

....The wind sweeps the land like a giant broom.....

Watch the freckled friends in frivolous frolic.

A train is a ferocious dragon that roars through the night.

As the sun smiles down on earth's children...

A butterfly is a flower blooming in the sky.

Listen to the oosh-whosh-sshush of the giant power wheels.

The startled bees buzzed angrily.

The tree spreads her leafy arm to shade the weary traveler.

U<small>FO</small>s

Name _____

Using what you have learned on the first UFO page, create additional ones to match each identifying shield shown here.

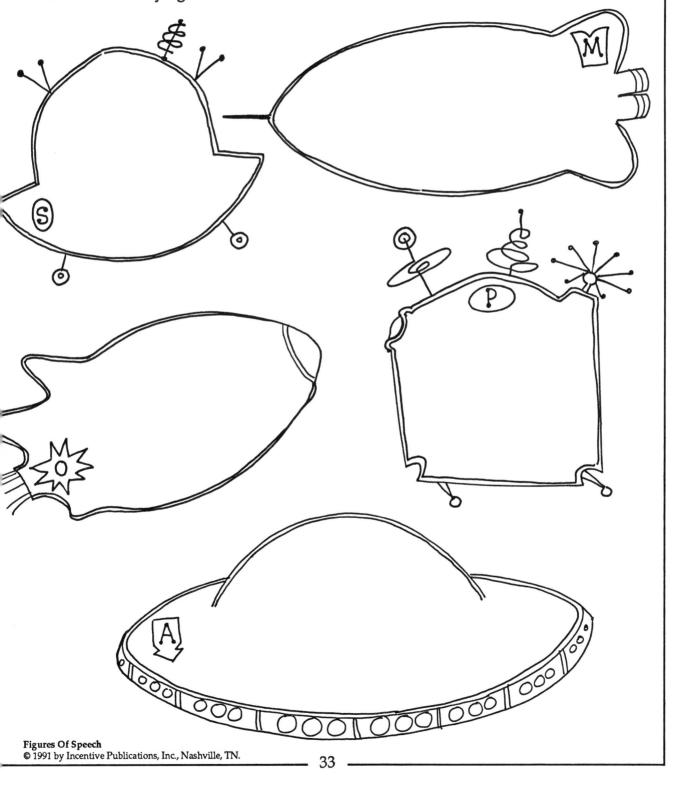

LITERARY LINGO

PURPOSE:
Identifying figures of speech and literary terms

PREPARATION:

1. Prepare 8 posters with one of the following titles on each:

Metaphor	Simile	Alliteration	Personification
Idioms	Puns	Hyperbole	Onomatopoeia

Add at least one example to each poster as a "starter," and display the posters together on a large bulletin board.

2. Provide a stack of old newspapers and magazines. (*Sports Illustrated*, *McCall's*, *Ladies Home Journal*, *Seventeen*, and daily papers are especially good for this activity.)

3. Reproduce a copy of the LITERARY LINGO work sheet for each student.

PROCEDURE:

1. Direct students to search the papers and magazines for examples of each of the literary terms and to paste their findings on the appropriate posters.

2. Leave completed posters on display so that students may become familiar with many examples of these literary terms.

3. At a subsequent time, give each student a copy of the LITERARY LINGO work sheet. Direct students to fill in each poster with as many original examples of each literary term as possible.

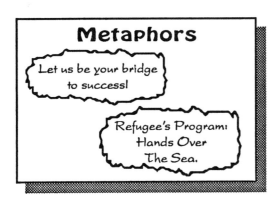

Metaphors

Let us be your bridge to success!

Refugee's Program: Hands Over The Sea.

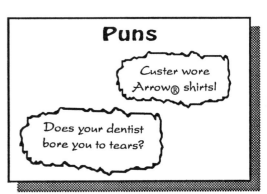

Puns

Custer wore Arrow® shirts!

Does your dentist bore you to tears?

LITERARY LINGO

Name _____

Make this miniature bulletin board come alive with your own original figures of speech and examples of literary terms.

PUN

PERSONIFICATION

IDIOM

SIMILE

METAPHOR

OMATOPOEIA

HYPERBOLE

ALLITERATION

Figures of Speech, Literary Terms
© 1991 by Incentive Publications, Inc., Nashville, TN.

AS SMART AS A WHIP

Name _____

Are you? Prove it. See if you can complete these similes.

As fresh as as _____   As neat as a _____

As meek as a _____   As blind as a _____

As good as _____   As cool as a _____

As sly as a _____   As dead as a _____

As sweet as a _____   As stubborn as a _____

As clear as _____   As pale as a _____

As quick as a _____   As funny as a _____

As clean as a _____   As pretty as a _____

How did a whip get to be smart? In these spaces, copy four of your favorite similes from the list above. Beside each, write your guess as to how this simile came to be a common figure of speech.

_____ - _____

_____

_____ - _____

_____

_____ - _____

_____

_____ - _____

_____

Some of the similes above have been around a long time and are pretty worn out. On another sheet of paper, make up some sparkling new similes of your own. Make them fun to share with your classmates!

Similes
© 1991 by Incentive Publications, Inc., Nashville, TN.

A PROBLEM OF PERSPECTIVE

Name _____

    A very well-known poet named Shel Silverstein created a poem in which he pretended he was writing from inside a lion. It changed the normal climate or position from which he would be writing.

    Try writing a short poem or mini-story from each of these unusual "climates."

…from inside a bottle

…from inside a volcano

…from atop the cherry on the world's largest hot fudge sundae

…from underneath Big Foot's foot

PUN FUN

Name _____

Every good writer is in love with words and enjoys the humor associated with words and word games. A pun is a play on words such as is demonstrated in the match game below. See if you can match each speaker with the appropriate quote.

____ 1. owner of a cleaning establishment

____ 2. cannibal

____ 3. veterinarian

____ 4. lawyer

____ 5. kindergarten teacher

____ 6. dentist

____ 7. middle grade teacher

____ 8. night watchperson

____ 9. astronomer

____ 10. farmer

____ 11. nuclear scientist (on vacation)

____ 12. surgeon

a. "A lost puppy is a dog gone."

b. "I'll keep you in stitches!"

c. "Just in case..."

d. "Gene fission."

e. "I love all people."

f. "I try to make little things count."

g. "Sow what."

h. "I have a pressing engagement."

i. "My business is looking up."

j. "My occupation is very filling."

k. "I've never done a day's work!"

l. "My students have no class!"

Now take your turn at being a punster by creating an original pun of your own. Try it on your friends and fellow writers! (By the way, would you call a gentleman who was fond of making puns "pungent"?)

My Best Pun Yet:

_____

_____

1. h; 2. e; 3. a; 4. c; 5. f; 6. j;
7. l; 8. k; 9. i; 10. g; 11. d; 12. b

EGG-OMANIA

Egg-omania is "cracking" people up! They are putting one "over easy" on their friends!

See how many of the eggs you can "unscramble."

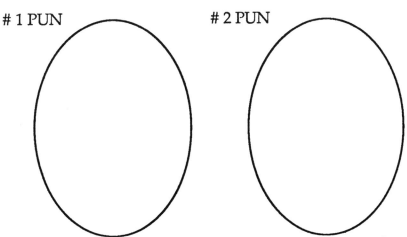

"Eggs" + "Hit" = "Eggs-Hit," or EXIT!

. ⬭ + Salt = _____   5. ⬭ + Sam = _____

.. ⬭ + 🥑 = _____   6. ⬭ + ⛺ = _____

. ⬭ + ✈ = _____   7. ⬭ + 👓 = _____

:. ⬭ + 🪙 = _____   8. ⬭ + LB = _____

The sentences at the top of this page use puns. Look up the meaning of the word pun in the dictionary. Then use the space here to write a pun or two of your own!

1 PUN

2 PUN

Answer Key: 1. exalt; 2. excel; 3. explain; 4. exchange; 5. exam; 6. extent; 7. excise; 8. expound

DO YOU SPEAK SPORTS?

Name _____

    Many areas of interest have their own special jargon (or group of vocabulary words). In writing about these things, a writer must be able to use this jargon skillfully and accurately.

    Each illustration below suggests an area of interest that has its own special jargon. Fill the spaces provided with as many of these related words as possible. (Encyclopedias, dictionaries, magazines, and books related to these topics will be of great help.)

FASHION

_____
_____
_____
_____

BALL GAMES

inning
mound
_____
_____

HORSES

dressage
_____
_____
_____

CARS

pit stop
_____
_____
_____

MUSIC

_____
_____
_____
_____

    Using one of the lists you have created, write a brief newspaper article describing an event in that area of interest. Write your article on scrap paper. Edit and refine it. Then copy it onto another sheet of paper.

Jargon
© 1991 by Incentive Publications, Inc., Nashville, TN.

JUKEBOX JARGON

Name _____

    Did you ever hear of the song *Love Your Lazy Liver* sung by Limp Lung and the Laplanders? No? Well, neither did anyone else. All that song has going for it is **a lot of alliteration.** (How about that?)

    This jukebox plays only hit songs with alliterative titles, sung by alliterative artists. The key buttons give you the initial sound for each record. You get to name the tunes and the artists.

SK _____

B _____

W _____

TR _____

J _____

D _____

M _____

FL _____

R _____

ST _____

Write the name of your favorite "hit." Be prepared to share both title and artist!

_____

Alliteration
© 1991 by Incentive Publications, Inc., Nashville, TN.

PURPOSE:
Using sensory appeal

PREPARATION:

1. Ask students to close their eyes and picture in their minds the most delicious foods they can imagine.

2. Then, ask them to think of words and phrases they might use to describe the foods. Write these on the chalkboard as they are suggested. Try to fill the entire board with words and phrases that have sensory appeal.

3. Provide a copy of the MEAL APPEAL work sheet for each student along with various colors of construction paper, paste, scissors, and crayons.

PROCEDURE:

1. Students color, cut out, and use the food pictures from the work sheet to create a MEAL APPEAL menu. Direct them to name and price the items and to create a restaurant name to be used as the title for the menu.

2. Beside each picture, students should describe the item in terms that are so strong in sensory appeal that they make the reader's digestive juices begin to flow. (The words collected on the chalkboard can be used for reference.)

3. Collect the finished menus, and display them for all to enjoy.

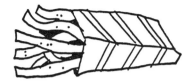

Cut out these pictures and use them to make your menu.
Don't forget to give each item a name and a price, and put the name of your restaurant on the menu!

Sensory Appeal
© 1991 by Incentive Publications, Inc., Nashville, TN.

AD ANALYST

PURPOSE:
Using emotional appeal

PREPARATION:

1. Write the following four phrases on the chalkboard.
- appeal to sentiment
- appeal to desire for status or success
- appeal to desire for adventure
- appeal to sense of economy

2. Reproduce and provide a copy of the ad page for each student.

3. Provide dictionaries and a variety of magazines for reference.

4. Prepare bulletin board space to accommodate a collage of magazine ads, and provide scissors, paste, and construction paper for mounting and display purposes.

PROCEDURE:

1. Make certain that students understand the meaning of each phrase on the board. They can use dictionaries to check the definitions if necessary.

2. Direct students to study the page of ads carefully to try to understand the intent or purpose of each one.

3. Students then write one or more of the four purposes on the line provided beneath each ad.

4. Students circle the key word or words in each ad that helped most in understanding the intent of the ad.

5. Then ask students to peruse magazines to locate an example of each of the four kinds of advertising.

6. Students should cut and mount each ad example on colorful construction paper, label it using one of the four identifying phrases, and add it to the prepared bulletin board display.

uiet Quality

...cause you enjoy being first-class.

How do you say,
"Thank-You"
to someone
you love?

from...Happy Days Gift Shop

Place yourself in ecstacy

...without leaving
your pocketbook in agony
Luxury Island Vacations

This is no vacation spot
for the weak at heart.

SUNSHINE MOUNTAIN EXPEDITIONS

Guaranteed to
take you away
from it all!

WHO'S THE VILLAIN?

Name _____

    Has it ever occurred to you that the story of *The Three Little Pigs* might possibly make the big, bad wolf look like the villain when he really wasn't? Think about the poor old wolf who was teased, taunted, and finally killed by the pigs. What about his side of the story?

    Pretend that you are a newspaper reporter who got to talk to the wolf before he died. On the lines below, write your account of the story as it might have appeared in the local paper the day after the wolf died. Don't forget your headline! Add a picture too!

Village News   25

Big Bad Wolf

_____

_____

_____

_____

_____

_____

_____

_____

_____

_____

_____

_____

_____

_____

_____

_____

_____

_____

Point Of View
© 1991 by Incentive Publications, Inc., Nashville, TN.

WHEN A BAG IS NOT A BAG

hat
mask
basket
bib
place mat
boxing gloves

PURPOSE:
Developing imagery and imagination

PREPARATION:

1. Use brown paper bags with a single object inside each.

2. As an example, hold up one bag, take out the object, and lead a class discussion centered on possible uses for the object other than its normal use. Encourage imaginative and unusual responses. List suggested uses on the board, and continue discussion in a fun but no-nonsense setting so long as spontaneous contributions are being offered.

3. Repeat the process with the bag itself.

4. Then ask students to follow the directions below.

PROCEDURE:

1. Select one bag each.

2. List as many uses for the object inside the bag as you can. S–T–R–E–T–C–H your mind for new and different ones.

3. At the end of ten minutes, the person with the longest list of uses for his/her object is declared the winner of the game and gets to read his/her list to the group.

4. All lists could be placed in the bag with the proper object, bags arranged on a table, and for the next few days, students can enjoy looking at the objects and adding to the lists.

JUST FOR FUN

How many uses can you think of for...

a tennis shoe	a dinner fork
a lily pad	a strand of hair
your desk	a button

MOOD OVER MIAMI

Name _____

Miami, Florida, has long enjoyed a reputation as a romantic city. Each year, thousands of people from all over the world flock to Miami beaches for holiday relaxation and fun. But Miami, as any large city, also has its sinister side. It has crime, violence, and racial unrest – all the tensions of a world-class population center.

Pretend you are a writer who has chosen Miami as the setting for your next novel. As a good novelist, you will write sentences that create mood and are full of imagery. In the spaces below, write the opening sentence for a chapter of your Miami-based novel – one for each of the moods suggested below.

A foreboding, eerie, or scary mood

A jovial mood

A mood of peace and tranquility

A mood of suspense

A mood of excitement or anticipation

Mood, Imagery
© 1991 by Incentive Publications, Inc., Nashville, TN.

HYPERBOLE HYSTERIA

Name _____

Hyper-what? Do you know how to pronounce that word? Do you know what it means? Haven't you been told at least a million times to look up words you don't know? Well, look it up. Mark its pronunciation and write its definition in the space below. Then, underline the hyperbole in this paragraph.

HYPERBOLE – _____
_____

See, all those million pieces of advice paid off!

Below are 32 phrases or sentences. Some of them are hyperboles; others are not. Circle the number of each hyperbole.

1. A rolling stone gathers no moss.
2. I'm so hungry I could eat a horse.
3. Well, I'll be a monkey's uncle!
4. His head's as big as a barrel.
5. I've told you a million times not to do that.
6. Haste makes waste.
7. Your suitcase weighs a ton!
8. One, two, buckle my shoe.
9. He could write his autobiography on the head of a pin.
10. That snake was a mile long.
11. My mind was going in a thousand different directions.
12. If that's so, I'll eat my hat.
13. That baby is as light as a feather.
14. Rise and shine!
15. My new jeans cost a fortune!
16. If I ate that much, I'd be as big as a house.
17. Early to bed, early to rise…
18. May I sew you to a sheet?
19. Oh, Mable, I haven't seen you for at least a hundred years!
20. She moves slower than a glacier.
21. He talks ninety miles an hour.
22. It took me forever to read that book.
23. He runs faster than a speeding bullet.

On another sheet of paper, write one original hyperbole related to each subject below:

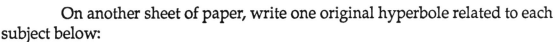

your family   food   your body   schoolwork   the future

Hyperbole
© 1991 by Incentive Publications, Inc., Nashville, TN.

CAN YOU TELL CHARACTER BY ITS COVER?

Name _____

    Carefully observe each of the three characters below. Think about what kind of person each might be. Now ask yourself what things about the character's appearance helped you decide what this person might be like.

    In the circle beside each character, write a group of characteristics which describe that person. Then in the box by each, write a paragraph describing something the person does that will demonstrate those characteristics.

RETOLD TALES

PURPOSE:
Writing dialogue

PREPARATION:

1. Acquire several books which include stories that can be dramatized. (Old favorites such as *Three Billy Goats Gruff*, *The Little Red Hen*, *The Three Little Pigs*, *Little Red Riding Hood*, and *Goldilocks and the Three Bears* will work well.)

2. Provide a "good stuff junk box" full of old scarves, hats, paper bags, construction paper, scissors, paste, etc. Students can use these materials for prop and costume construction.

3. Divide students into small groups, and direct each group to select a story to be dramatized by following the procedure directions.

PROCEDURE:

Read and discuss the story selected.

1. Make a list of all the characters in the story.

2. Give the story a modern setting, and change the characters of the story accordingly.

3. Write the story in play form.

4. Use materials from the "good stuff junk box" to make costumes.

5. Stage your play as a TV special and present it to the rest of the class.

DESCRIPTIONS BY DESIGN

Name _____

Many companies mail catalogs by the thousands to customers all over the world. The descriptions given for the catalog items pictured are very important since they may actually determine the customer's decision to order or not order an item.

On a separate sheet of paper, write brief paragraphs describing each of the items pictured below. Begin each paragraph with a catchy sentence to capture the reader's attention. Cut out the pictures, and paste them on the DESCRIPTIONS BY DESIGN work sheet. Copy each of your descriptive paragraphs beside its corresponding picture to make a page for a toy catalog.

A.

B.
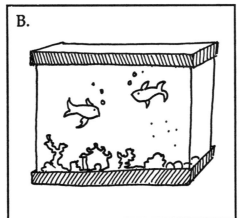

C.
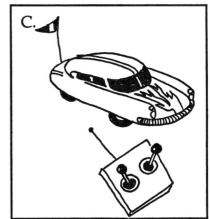

D.

E.

F.

EVERYTHING I ALWAYS WANTED!

Descriptions
© 1991 by Incentive Publications, Inc., Nashville, TN.

DESCRIPTIONS BY DESIGN

Name _____

A.

B.

C.

A. _____

_____

_____

_____

B. _____

_____

_____

_____

C. _____

_____

_____

_____

D.

E.

D. _____

_____

E. _____

_____

F.

F. _____

_____

_____

_____

SILLY-NILLY STORIES

PURPOSE:
Writing a narrative story

PREPARATION:

1. Provide lots of old magazines, scissors, paste, large sheets of construction paper, and pencils.

2. Prepare two or three "Silly-Nilly" pictures to be used as starters (see directions on the MAKE A SILLY-NILLY work sheet).

3. Paste the directions on a sheet of folded cardboard to make a study guide.

4. Place the materials in a free-choice interest center.

5. Make a "Silly-Nilly Stories" caption, and prepare a bulletin board near the center.

MAKE A SILLY-NILLY

1. Make your own "Silly-Nilly" by cutting parts from two or three magazine pictures to put together to make one "crazy, couldn't be true" illustration. (Examples: a school bus loaded with children with the driver cut out and replaced by a hippopotamus; children on a picnic with one child replaced by a mermaid; an airplane in midair with its wings replaced by angel or butterfly wings.)

2. Look through the magazine to find parts for your own "Silly-Nilly." Compose your "Silly-Nilly" carefully, and paste it on the top part of a sheet of construction paper.

3. Write a story to go with your "Silly-Nilly." Think about your characters, and make up a plot to go with them. Try to give your story a dramatic or surprise ending.

4. Write your story on scratch paper first; then copy it over carefully.

5. Add your story to the "Silly-Nilly" bulletin board.

Narrative
© 1991 by Incentive Publications, Inc., Nashville, TN.

THE "BEAR" FACTS

Name _____

News reporters know that their readers want the facts. They must report them without extra words or ideas and without adding their own opinions about what happened.

Pretend you were the reporter sent to investigate the story of *Goldilocks and the Three Bears,* and gather the facts you need so you can write the story. Use the information file card to organize your facts. Then, in the lined space below, write the story as it might have appeared in the *Bearville Banner.*

Reporter's Information File Card

What happened? _____
_____

Who did something?_____

When did it happen? _____

Where did it happen?_____

Why or **how** did it happen?_____
_____

Bearville Banner

5¢

Today's new
yesterday's

_____
_____
_____
_____
_____
_____
_____
_____
_____
_____
_____
_____
_____
_____
_____
_____
_____
_____

THE "BEAR" FACTS

Name _____

    You probably read the following bear stories when you were very young. Refresh your memory by rereading them, and make an information file card for each one. (If you can't locate the stories in the library, use what you remember and create additional facts to supplement, or make up complete stories of your own about these characters.)

How the Bear Lost His Tail

at happened? _____
   or
_____

o did something?_____

en did it happen? _____

ere did it happen? _____

y or **how** did it happen?_____
_____

Pooh Gets Into a Tight Place

What happened? _____
    or
_____

Who did something?_____

When did it happen? _____

Where did it happen? _____

Why or **how** did it happen?_____
_____

Paddington Bear

at happened? _____
   or
_____

o did something?_____

en did it happen? _____

ere did it happen? _____

y or **how** did it happen?_____
_____

BONUS:

Using what you have learned about collecting the "bear" facts and composing new stories, make up a brief news story – funny or serious – about one of the following:

dancer, **"Bear"yshnikov**
U.S. Bear Force
team, **Chicago Bears**
Soviet leader, **Mikhail Gor"bear"chev**
composer, **Ludvig Von"Bear"hoven**
    city of **"Bear"ut**
    singer, **"Bear"y Manilow**
    city of **"Bear" lin**
    your "Beary" own choice!

News Reporting
© 1991 by Incentive Publications, Inc., Nashville, TN.

RHYME IN TIME

Name _____

The rhythm of poetry makes it especially fun to say and hear. Often, the last words of the lines form a rhyming pattern.

Read these poems, and use matching colors to underline the lines that rhyme. Then, mark the lines that are the same color with the same letter.

The day I **tried**   A
To eat a whole cake.   B
I nearly **died**   A
Of a stomachache!   B

I beg you, please,   ____
Try not to sneeze.   ____
It makes a breeze,   ____
And spreads disease!   ____

Candy   ____
Is dandy!   ____
Stew…   ____
Phew!   ____

A guy who needs some math help   ____
Can buy a fine computer,   ____
But tricky math can also   ____
Be taught by a personal tutor.   ____

On a morning hung heavy with fog   ____
Quite early, I went for a jog.   ____
  Still mostly asleep,   ____
  I neglected to leap,   ____
And landed my head on a log!   ____

Nothing on this planet beats a   ____
Cheese and pepperoni pizza…   ____
ONE is NOT enough!   ____
Tell me, what is more delightful   ____
Than a scrumptious, deep dish biteful   ____
Of that stringy stuff?   ____

Rhyme Schemes
© 1991 by Incentive Publications, Inc., Nashville, TN.

HERE'S THE TIME...
YOU MAKE THE RHYME!

Name _____

Write a rhyming poem on each of the line sets below. Make the rhyming lines in your poem match the rhyme patterns marked, and make one set of the rhyming words rhyme with the time shown on the nearest clock.

Example:

If there's ever a poet,	A
The poet is you!	B
So please write some poems	C
To show what you can do.	B

_____ A
_____ B
_____ A
_____ B

_____ A
_____ A
_____ B
_____ B

_____ A
_____ B
_____ C
_____ B

_____ A
_____ A
_____ A
_____ A

LOVIN' LIMERICKS

Name _____

In a boggy old marsh by the sea   _____
Sat a frog on a log lonesomely.   _____
There in his own shade   _____
He spied a mermaid   _____
And coaxed her to sit on his knee.   _____

That is a lovin' limerick!

Do you know what makes a poem a limerick? First, it must have a special rhyme scheme. The first two lines rhyme with each other, the second two lines with each other, and the last line rhymes with the first two lines. This rhyme scheme is written a-a-b-b-a.

Label the rhyme scheme in the lovin' limerick above by writing the correct letters in the correct spaces.

A limerick also has a special rhythm pattern.

Line 1 has 3 accented syllables.
Line 2 has 3 accented syllables.
Line 3 has 2 accented syllables.   Read the above limerick aloud.
Line 4 has 2 accented syllables.   Can you hear the special
Line 5 has 3 accented syllables.   rhythm pattern?

Use this space to write pairs or groups of rhyming words that could be used in writing lovin' limericks. A few are listed for you:

mine	love	marry	care	keep	heart
fine	dove	Harry	fair	leap	apart
Valentine	above	tarry	hair	weep	dart
merry	pair	you	dear	_____	_____
cherry	rare	blue	tear	_____	_____
very	stare	too	near	_____	_____

_____ _____ _____ _____
_____ _____ _____ _____
_____ _____ _____ _____
_____ _____ _____ _____

LOVIN' LIMERICKS

Name _____

Use your groups of rhyming words to create a special limerick about each of these lovin' pairs. (You may ignore the suggestion you like least and substitute one of your own!)

A freckle and a hair

Peanut butter & jelly

A kid and a pizza

A book and bookworm

A shoe and a foot

POETRY YOU CAN EAT

PURPOSE:
Writing haikus, cinquains, and free verse

PREPARATION:

1. Bring to the classroom a variety of fruits and vegetables that can be eaten raw – at least one piece for each student.

2. Provide a copy of the poetry work sheets for each student, a pencil, a sheet of writing paper, and an appropriate environment for a creative writing activity.

PROCEDURE:

1. Each student chooses a piece of fruit or a vegetable.

2. The student then follows these instructions given by the teacher.

1. Write three words that tell how your food looks.
2. Write two words that describe its shapes.
3. Hold the food in one hand, close your eyes, and rub it gently with the other hand. Write a word that describes its texture.
4. Close your eyes again. Smell your food. Write two words that describe its fragrance.
5. Take a bite. Write a sound word that describes what you heard when you bit it.
6. Write two similes that tell how it feels in your mouth and on your tongue.
7. Write three adjectives that describe its taste.
8. Write a line that personifies the fruit or vegetable.
9. Name a person or thing this object reminds you of, and tell why.
10. If you could rename this fruit or vegetable, what appropriate name would you give it?

3. After following the instructions, the student uses that information to complete the HAIKU HIBACHI, ODE TO AN ORANGE, and VEGGIES IN THE VERNACULAR work sheets.

HAIKU HIBACHI

Name _____

The Japanese invented a very beautiful form of poetry called haiku. It is unrhymed, has three lines, and refers in some way to one of the seasons of the year.

Your fruit or vegetable is a very special product of one of those seasons. Use this Japanese hibachi to "cook up" a haiku about your fruit or vegetable, and write it below. Don't forget to add a hint of the correct season.

Remember, in a haiku, line 1 must have five syllables; line 2 must have seven syllables; and line 3 must have five syllables.

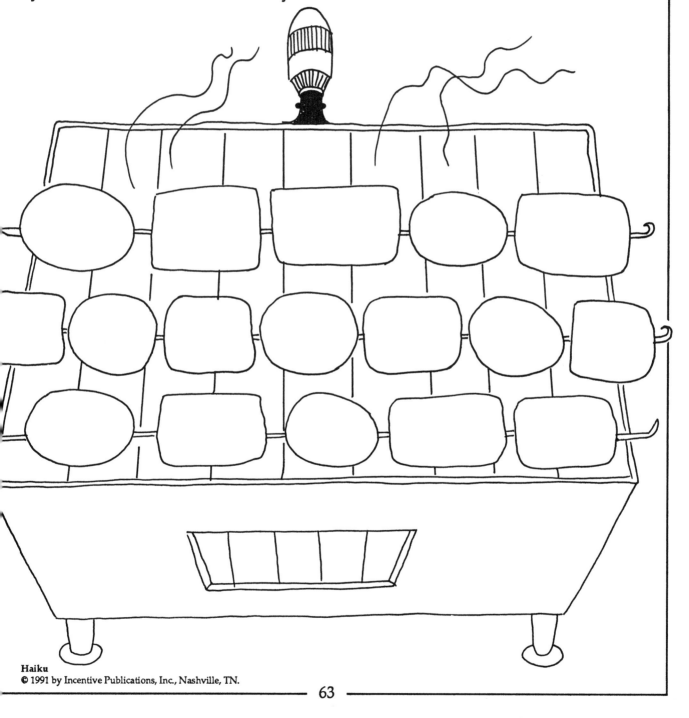

ODE TO AN ORANGE

Name _____

> orange
> tangy, sweet
> eat, drink, squirt
> fragrant like spring blossoms
> Sunshine!

This form of poetry is called cinquain. Its characteristic features are:

Line 1 – one word, a subject or an idea
Line 2 – two words, adjectives describing the subject
Line 3 – three words, verbs related to subject
Line 4 – four words, telling your reaction to subject
Line 5 – one word, a synonym for the subject

Take a special look at your fruit or vegetable. Reread the words you have collected during the first part of this activity. Then, pretend that your fruit or vegetable has some human qualities.

Write a poetic tribute in cinquain form here to honor it.	Write a humorous cinquain here about the same food.

VEGGIES IN THE VERNACULAR

Name _____

Pineapples in the sky
Cherries jubilee riding high
Bananas Flambé in sunset colors
Whipped cream mountains
    with marmalade peaks
And a strawberry breeze...
    Fruit float!

That's a free verse – poetry that has a certain flowing rhythm but no regular pattern of rhyme. It's fun to write because it frees the poet to use language just as he/she wishes.

In each food shape below, write a short free verse poem that gives your own special impression about that food.

Free Verse
© 1991 by Incentive Publications, Inc., Nashville, TN.

FUN WITH PHOETRY*

PURPOSE:
Writing quatrains and diamantés

PREPARATION:

1. Review with the students the definitions and features of the quatrain and the diamanté poetry forms.

Quatrain–any four-line poem

Example:

A quatrain has poetic words
Grouped in lines – just four.
Fewer, not allowed at all...
And never, never more!

Diamanté–a seven-line poem whose lines create a diamond shape

Rules	**Example**
Line 1 – one noun or pronoun	Diamanté
Line 2 – two adjectives	shaped, unusual
Line 3 – three participles	exciting, entertaining, intriguing
Line 4 – four nouns	thought, creation, harmony, description
Line 5 – three participles	challenging, satisfying, lasting
Line 6 – two adjectives	precise, brief
Line 7 – one noun (usually a synonym for the first line)	Poem.

2. Provide magazines, paste, scissors, pens, and construction paper.

PROCEDURE:

1. Each student looks through a magazine to find two photographs. He/she cuts out one in a rectangular or square shape and one in a diamond shape, and pastes these on light-colored construction paper.

2. The student creates a quatrain and writes it around the four edges of the square-cut photograph. Then the student creates a diamanté, writes it on a small, diamond-shaped piece of paper, and pastes it in the center of the diamond-shaped photo.

3. Students share and display their completed work.

*A combination of poetry and photographs

RING AROUND THE COUPLET

PURPOSE:
Creating couplets

PREPARATION:

1. Reproduce the game board on the following pages and paste inside a file folder or onto stiff paper.

2. Trace a quarter to make two circles. Leave one white, and shade the other to match the shaded circles on the game board. Paste these two circles to the two sides of a quarter.

3. Place the game board, the quarter, and some buttons of different colors (to be used as markers) where students may have free access to them.

PROCEDURE:

1. Two students choose markers and place them on "start."

2. The first student tosses the quarter and moves the marker to the nearest ring that matches the "up" side of the quarter.

3. The student must then create a couplet using the two rhyming words which appear in that ring. (Remind students that the lines of a couplet must not only rhyme but match in the number of accented syllables.)

4. If the student cannot create a couplet using the given words, he/she remains on that spot but forfeits the next turn.

5. After the first student finishes his/her turn, the second student tosses the quarter, moves accordingly, and tries to make a couplet.

6. The game continues in this manner until one player reaches the "goal" to win the game.

Name _____

START

DAY
STAY

MORE
SORE

HAIR
BEAR

GO
FLOW

CRY
FRY

CUP
UP

EIGHT
LATE

WOOD
STOOD

HAD
DAD

sniff

Name _____

TITLE TALE

PURPOSE:
Writing titles

PREPARATION:

1. Secure duplicate copies of magazines appropriate to the age and interest level of the students.

2. Cut out articles from one of the magazines. Remove the titles, and place each article in a separate envelope or manila folder.

3. Place the envelopes, pencils, paper, and the uncut magazine in a free-choice interest center. Add a study guide giving the procedure directions.

PROCEDURE:

1. Select an envelope, and read the magazine article inside.

2. On a sheet of paper, write one to three sentences that give the main idea of the article.

3. Quickly skim the article again to make sure you have captured the main idea.

4. Write an interesting title for the article that you feel is representative of the main idea and that would also encourage someone to read the article.

5. Now, check the title in the magazine to see how your title compares with the original.

BEAT THE PUBLISHER

PURPOSE:
Writing titles, subtitles, and captions

PREPARATION:

1. Find 2 copies of a specific issue of a newspaper or magazine.

2. Choose several articles from the publication, and cut them from each copy. Cut the articles apart at each place where a subtitle or caption appears. Then, clip off all titles, subtitles, and captions from the articles, and place the pieces in envelopes (one for each article). Attach each envelope to another envelope containing its matching, uncut article.

3. Give each student one or more envelope sets, a marking pen, white construction paper, and paste or tape.

PROCEDURE:

1. Each student takes the article pieces from the marked envelope and reads them carefully. He/she then puts the parts of the article in order and pastes them on the construction paper leaving space between each article part.

2. The student then writes a title for the article and adds subtitles or captions (for pictures) in the spaces between each article part.

3. When the task is completed, the student may look in the other envelope to see the original title and subtitles for the article and to compare those with his/her own.

4. The student decides which he/she thinks is better – the original or his/her own – and writes a brief memo to the teacher expressing and supporting his/her opinion.

THE INCREDIBLE PROOF PRINCE

Name _____

Unfortunately, the Proof Prince had to be out of the kingdom today.

Unfortunately, the Duke of Error has a young cousin who has created some trouble spots.

Fortunately, the prince has a friend like you who can use his magic prints to wipe out the trouble. Use the prince's proofreader's "prints" to correct the errors in the story.

THE PRINCE'S MAGIC PRINTS

˅	.... insert apostrophe
⌐	.... delete
c̲	.... make capital
/	.... make lowercase
◡	.... close up space
(sp)	.... spell out
⊙	.... insert period
⋀	.... insert comma
˅/˅	.... insert quotation marks
¶ or ∟	.... begin new paragraph

THE INCREDIBLE PROOF PRINCE

Name _____

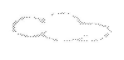

Once there was a Valiant prince who traveled the Kingdom of the Written Word making wrong things write he was called the Incredible Proof Prince because he made it his business to ferret our trouble here and there always leaving one of his special magic points on an exact trouble spot causing it to turn out just write.

he was loved by every one in the Kingdom – everyone except the Duke of Error. The Duke was a rotten fellow who did what he could to cast evil spellings and cause mis understandings he even resorted to defacing distorting and destroying road signs so that travelers would become hopelessly lost and confused the Kingdom was miserable.

Finally, the incredible proof prince could stand it no longer he became enraged and shouted out out with Error! Nevermore shall you cause confusion in this kingdom! With that he drew his powerful proofreaders pen-sword and reduced the Duke of Error to an ordinary lower-case duke, no longer heralded by staunch exclamation points, but left handing by freying threads to the coat tail of a cowardly question mark.

Long live the Incredible Proof Prince!

Proofreading
© 1991 by Incentive Publications, Inc., Nashville, TN.

THE WRITER'S BEST FRIEND

PURPOSE:
Editing

PREPARATION:

1. Locate a variety of newspaper and magazine articles which may be cut out and pasted on student work pages.

2. Provide at least two of the following kinds of articles for each student:

1. a brief news, feature, or editorial item.
2. a longer narrative magazine article.

3. Reproduce a copy of the EDITOR'S REVIEW for each student.

4. Discuss the role of the editor – one who critiques a piece of writing. Talk about the kinds of things an editor thinks about or looks for. Make the point that a writer's best friend is the editor even though the editor may also be the writer's harshest critic because he/she helps to make the finished product better. Also point out that self-editing is one of the best things a writer can learn to do.

5. Hand out copies of the EDITOR'S REVIEW, and discuss the questions so that students will know how to use the guide effectively.

PROCEDURE:

1. Distribute news and magazine articles to the students. Direct them to attach them to sheets of notebook paper.

2. Students then use the EDITOR'S REVIEW as a guide for "editing" the articles and sharpening their own technical writing skills.

EDITOR'S REVIEW

Name _____

Who wrote this article? _____

Who was his/her intended audience? _____

Do you think the piece appeals to that audience? _____

What response does the writer hope for? _____
_____

In your opinion, has the writer included enough information and presented his/her idea well enough to get that response?_____ Explain. _____
_____

Did the first few sentences attract your attention? _____

Was the writer's message easy to follow and understand? _____

Does the article end with a feeling or idea that leaves the reader with something to think about or make the reader glad that he/she has spent time reading the piece?
_____

Has the writer used clear, accurate, easily-understood words? _____

Underline the words or phrases in the article that could have been left out without changing any meanings.

Circle any overworked words or phrases.

Count the number of sentences that begin with "there" or "it." Rewrite one of the sentences here. _____
_____

Find the longest or most complicated sentence in the article. Rewrite the same thought here in shorter sentences. _____
_____

Did you like the writer's style? _____

Might you have chosen to read this article even if your teacher had not required it?
_____ Why or why not? _____
_____

These are some of the kinds of questions a good writer asks himself/herself when he/she edits his/her own writing. Keep this page handy to use as you edit future assignments.

Editing
© 1991 by Incentive Publications, Inc., Nashville, TN.

BREAKING THE CONJUNCTION CHAIN

Name _____

Some people write sentences that just run on and on because they can't decide how to divide the sentences to make shorter, more easily read sentences, and they tell too many things or convey too many thoughts. This style of writing becomes hard to read, so the reader tends to just give up and refuses to try to get the message or even to read, what has been written. Do you know anyone who writes run-on sentences and therefore confuses the issue and actually bores the reader, or worse still, do you write run-on sentences yourself?

Rewrite the paragraph above dividing the sentences into shorter, more "readable" ones. Remember to present a complete thought in each sentence and to use correct punctuation.

_____
_____
_____
_____

_____
_____
_____
_____
_____
_____
_____
_____

List all the conjunctions that were left out in your rewriting.

_____
_____

Editing
© 1991 by Incentive Publications, Inc., Nashville, TN.

BIG IDEAS IN BRIEF

PURPOSE:
Exercising whole process writing skills – beginning to end!

PREPARATION:

1. Students will need pencils and paper and access to a dictionary, thesaurus, and any other word anthologies or references available.

2. Provide for each student one 3″ x 5″ index card.

PROCEDURE:

1. Write the following words on a chart or chalkboard:

greed	loneliness	hate	fear
youth	anger	change	anticipation
peace	freedom	joy	growth
tolerance	friendship	security	embarrassment

2. Ask students to choose the six ideas from the list above that intrigue them most and write them on paper, spaced widely apart.

3. First, using only their own mental resources and personal experiences, they should write beside each word all synonyms, antonyms, and other words they can associate with this word or idea.

4. Next, they should use a dictionary to further clarify and collect additional information associated with the word.

5. Finally, they should use the thesaurus and other word resource books to add to their store of knowledge about each word.

6. When they have completed this task, they should choose the one word or idea that interests them most and write about it using only as much space as is available on one side of a 3″ x 5″ card. Encourage them to express their strongest feelings and ideas about the chosen word in a few, precise, well-constructed sentences.

7. On the opposite side of the index card, students should write in large, block letters the word they have chosen and sign their name.

PEACE

8. Make a file of the cards for students to peruse and use for future reference in writing tasks.

Note: More able students may be encouraged to contribute more than one card to the file.

A MANY
SPLENDORED THING

PURPOSE:
Exercising whole process writing

PREPARATION:

1. Tear sheets of multicolored tissue paper into bits and pieces – the more shapes, sizes, and colors, the better. Maintain a free-form style with torn edges and no uniformity. Place the pieces in a basket or box.

2. Reproduce the A MANY SPLENDORED THING work sheet, and distribute it to the students along with glue and the following directions listed under "Procedure."

3. Prepare an appropriate display space where finished products may be shared.

PROCEDURE:

1. Close your eyes, reach into the basket, and take a good handful of paper bits.

2. Using only the bordered space on the A MANY SPLENDORED THING work sheet, arrange the paper bits to make a design. Let your imagination run free, and create the most original design possible before you glue it into place.

3. Look at your design. Give it a creative title, and list ten descriptive words and/or phrases that the design brings to mind.

4. Now, use scrap paper to create a song, poem, or story to go with your design. Ask a fellow writer to read, react to, and offer editing suggestions.

5. Refine and edit your written piece, copy it onto another sheet of paper, and attach it to your design.

A MANY SPLENDORED THING

Name _____

TEN EXCEPTIONALLY FINE DESCRIPTIVE WORDS & PHRASES

1. _____
2. _____
3. _____
4. _____
5. _____

6. _____
7. _____
8. _____
9. _____
10. _____

MASTERPIECE GALLERY

Name _____

You are about to create an artistic masterpiece using words and phrases as the images you will apply to your canvas.

You will need some old newspapers or magazines, scissors, paste, and a piece of heavy construction paper. Add a frame from another color of paper if you like.

Find at least one example of each item listed below. Then on your heavy paper, create a collage using the pieces you have collected.

When you have finished your collage, hang it where your classmates can see and enjoy your work.

- ❑ a caption
- ❑ an expletive
- ❑ a metaphor
- ❑ a possessive noun

- ❑ a title showing alliteration
- ❑ a phrase with a comma
- ❑ an interrogative sentence

- ❑ an adverb
- ❑ a proper noun
- ❑ an abbreviation
- ❑ a cliché

- ❑ a word unfamiliar to you (until now, of course)
- ❑ an imperative phrase or sentence
- ❑ a picture demonstrating personification

FACE IT!

ARMCHAIR TRAVELER

Solitary Silence

Festive

CHILI'S ON!

ANIMAL ANTICS

A ONE-DAY SEMINAR

WRAPPING UP THE SEASON

AF Sharpening Literary Competency Publications, Inc., Nashville, TN.
SWO# — 175891   PC# — 97
CUS# — 6776   DUE — 02/11